SKILLED AND VOCATIONAL TRADES

BECOME AN INDUSTRIAL MECHANIC

by Martha Hubbard

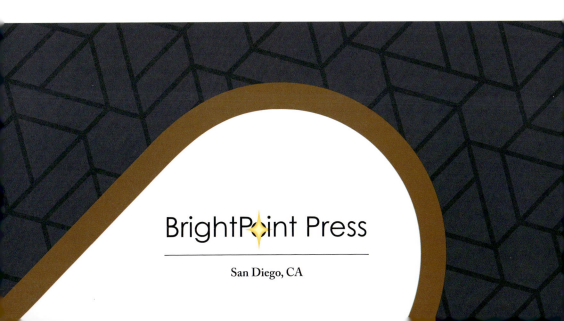

BrightPoint Press

San Diego, CA

© 2024 BrightPoint Press
an imprint of ReferencePoint Press, Inc.
Printed in the United States

For more information, contact:
BrightPoint Press
PO Box 27779
San Diego, CA 92198
www.BrightPointPress.com

ALL RIGHTS RESERVED.

No part of this work covered by the copyright hereon may be reproduced or used in any form or by any means—graphic, electronic, or mechanical, including photocopying, recording, taping, web distribution, or information storage retrieval systems—without the written permission of the publisher.

LIBRARY OF CONGRESS CATALOGING-IN-PUBLICATION DATA

Names: Hubbard, Martha, author.
Title: Become an industrial mechanic / by Martha Hubbard.
Description: San Diego, CA: BrightPoint Press, [2024] | Series: Skilled and vocational trades | Includes bibliographical references and index. | Audience: Ages 13 | Audience: Grades 7-9
Identifiers: LCCN 2023008680 (print) | LCCN 2023008681 (eBook) | ISBN 9781678206864 (hardcover) | ISBN 9781678206871 (eBook)
Subjects: LCSH: Industrial equipment--Maintenance and repair--Vocational guidance--Juvenile literature. | Mechanics (Persons)--Juvenile literature.
Classification: LCC TJ157 .H83 2024 (print) | LCC TJ157 (eBook) | DDC 621.023--dc23/eng/20230307
LC record available at https://lccn.loc.gov/2023008680
LC eBook record available at https://lccn.loc.gov/2023008681

CONTENTS

AT A GLANCE ... 4

INTRODUCTION ... 6
WHY BECOME AN INDUSTRIAL MECHANIC?

CHAPTER ONE ... 12
WHAT DOES AN
INDUSTRIAL MECHANIC DO?

CHAPTER TWO ... 26
WHAT TRAINING DO
INDUSTRIAL MECHANICS NEED?

CHAPTER THREE ... 38
WHAT IS LIFE LIKE AS AN
INDUSTRIAL MECHANIC?

CHAPTER FOUR ... 54
WHAT IS THE FUTURE FOR
INDUSTRIAL MECHANICS?

Glossary ... 74
Source Notes ... 75
For Further Research ... 76
Index ... 78
Image Credits ... 79
About the Author ... 80

AT A GLANCE

- Industrial mechanics work with large machinery. They keep machines running smoothly and must fix mechanical problems quickly.

- These workers may also be called industrial maintenance mechanics, production machinery mechanics, and maintenance technicians.

- Industrial mechanics work in many settings. For example, they can be found in food packaging plants, aircraft factories, large construction sites, and military facilities.

- Industrial mechanics usually work a typical forty-hour week. Overtime hours are sometimes required when there is a need.

- People can become an industrial mechanic without going to a four-year college. Apprenticeships, workforce training programs, and technical schools are some of the ways to train for this career.

- Those interested in a career as an industrial mechanic must enjoy working with their hands. They must be willing to keep learning as tools and technology change.

- There are many jobs available for industrial mechanics. The future is bright for this career.

- Advances in technology make this an exciting field for those with mechanical skills and a desire to learn.

INTRODUCTION

WHY BECOME AN INDUSTRIAL MECHANIC?

A large snack food production factory hums with activity. Railroad cars and trucks arrive in the morning. They come with fresh produce. Corn, potatoes, and oil are emptied onto a system of **conveyors**. Then they are moved to a large mixing room. The industrial mechanics make sure

In a snack factory, making sure every machine works smoothly is important.

the conveyors work properly. They do this so that the production process does not slow down or stop.

Next, the potatoes and corn are cooked, baked, or fried. The factory uses large fryers, ovens, and cooking pots to cook them. The fryers run on steam. The ovens use natural gas. The mechanics make sure that the gases are delivered to the processing room safely. This delivery system is **automated** by large computers. Specially trained mechanics carefully monitor these computers.

Once cooked, the fried snacks are seasoned. Mechanics make sure that the machinery is running constantly. Next, the seasoned snacks are packaged and boxed. Then, they go to a large warehouse. Robots and cranes transport, stack,

People who work near hot oil need to make sure they have the right safety equipment.

and load products. The snacks are then ready to be delivered to grocery stores. Mechanics work in every area of this large operation. Production factories rely on them. Mechanics keep every machine in working condition. They are the backbone of every industrial operation.

Industrial mechanics work with technology, including computer-controlled machines.

WHAT IS AN INDUSTRIAL MECHANIC?

Industrial mechanics work in many different industries. They can work in food processing, manufacturing, and energy plants. Mechanics maintain and repair large machines and other equipment. They must know how to use many types of tools and technology. Mechanics make sure that time and money are not lost.

A four-year college degree is not required for industrial mechanics. Trainees can apply for apprenticeships. This allows them to train on the job while getting paid. They can also go to trade schools or participate in workforce training programs. The future looks bright for industrial mechanics. Highly skilled workers are needed now more than ever.

CHAPTER ONE

WHAT DOES AN INDUSTRIAL MECHANIC DO?

Industrial mechanics maintain and repair large machinery and factory equipment. These machines make or package products. These products can include food and beverages. They can also include bigger products like engines and equipment used for construction.

Some industrial mechanics work in airplane factories.

Large manufacturing plants use teams of technicians and mechanics. Some companies might have several teams. Sometimes, mechanics will work with people in other departments.

Sharing information and working together to solve problems is essential. Communication is also important.

Mechanics are needed in a variety of industries. Some can be found working in electronics, defense, and medical manufacturing. In aviation, there

INDUSTRIAL MECHANICS AND MILLWRIGHTS: WHAT'S THE DIFFERENCE?

Sometimes job postings will refer to an industrial mechanic as a millwright. However, their job duties are different. An industrial mechanic maintains and repairs large machinery and equipment. A millwright dismantles, moves, and reassembles those machines. The two jobs sometimes overlap.

are machines that are used to build aircraft. In construction, large machinery must be maintained. Medical devices are made using specialized machines. In large production plants, food must be processed and packaged. Any industry that uses production, processing, and manufacturing equipment needs industrial mechanics.

Craig H. Hoffman is a manager at the Frito Lay plant in Perry, Georgia. He says that the mechanic's job is all about "automation, technology, and career opportunities."[1] Since technology is always improving, a mechanic's job

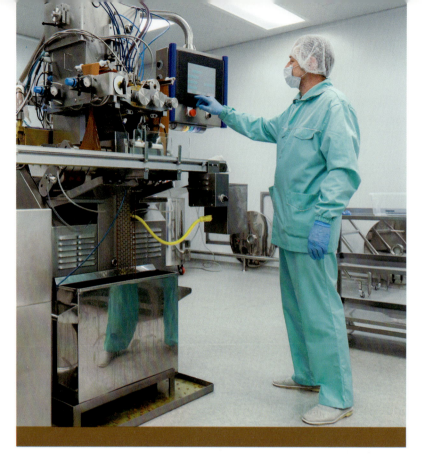

Mechanics who work in medical factories can keep things sterile, or free from bacteria, by wearing gloves and masks.

is constantly changing. Robots run by computers can be found at many facilities. Mechanics who know how to work with new technology are in demand. Those who have up-to-date training may take on more responsibility. This can mean they earn higher pay.

Mechanics have important work to do. They must repair and replace damaged mechanical parts. Machinery must be adjusted, cleaned, and oiled regularly. This is so that the machines work properly and efficiently. Mechanics run regular inspections for damage. Daily testing keeps equipment running at its best.

It is the mechanic's job to prevent problems before they occur. They do this by sticking to a regular maintenance schedule. In addition, industrial mechanics must keep good records. They must observe equipment and analyze test data.

At times, mechanics will have to use welding equipment. This is used to join metal objects together. They might also order materials and enter codes into computers. When mechanics gain more experience, they can train workers. They can assign duties. They can also plan employee work schedules.

A RESPECTED TEAM MEMBER

Mechanics are key members of large industrial operations. They typically work with other mechanics and

Industrial mechanics need to know how to work as a team.

technicians. But they can also work with

other departments. For example, they

sometimes work with the engineers who

design the machines. Mechanics must work to maintain the quality of all products.

The book *Career as an Industrial Maintenance Mechanic* states, "Since industrial maintenance mechanics have an intimate knowledge of the machinery and equipment at their facility, their advice is often sought before a company purchases new equipment."[2] Companies can save a lot of money if they can repair a machine instead of buying a new one. Complex machines can be expensive. A well-trained industrial mechanic is useful in these situations.

High school graduates can choose to go to vocational school or enter the workforce rather than going to a four-year college.

YOUNG PEOPLE IN THE SKILLED TRADES

The skilled trades are appreciated much more today than in the past. However, there is still a lack of education about trade careers, especially among young people. Skilled trade workers can earn a decent income, even when they start out. They work with cutting-edge technology. They are also in high demand. Many employers offer financial and educational benefits.

Shannon Brennan trained to be an industrial mechanic. She did an apprenticeship program in North Charleston, North Carolina. She now works with robotic machinery at Cummins Turbo Technologies. She is a manufacturing engineering technician.

Brennan was accepted into a work-study program while in high school. The program's goal was to train people in the skilled trades. The focus of many high schools is to prepare students for college. However, some students like Brennan go into the workforce after graduating.

Brennan's experience was very positive. She said, "I would go to Cummins for four hours a day and pretty much do on-the-job

THE MANUFACTURING SKILLS GAP

There is a serious shortage of people who are able to replace an aging workforce in the skilled trades. Mike Rowe hosted the *Dirty Jobs* television show. This show featured people with unusual jobs. Rowe provides competitive scholarships to help close this gap. Scholarship winners get their programs paid for by the mikeroweWORKS Foundation.

An apprenticeship is a great stepping stone into the field of industrial mechanics.

training and shadow people. I graduated my apprenticeship in April of 2016. I got offered a position full-time, so I'm no longer an apprentice."[3] When she got promoted to an engineering technician, Brennan was able to buy a house. Her company also paid for her to get an associate's degree.

CHAPTER TWO

WHAT TRAINING DO INDUSTRIAL MECHANICS NEED?

Industrial mechanics must have a high school diploma. A person who did not graduate high school can take a General Educational Development (GED) test. Passing the GED test can replace a high school diploma.

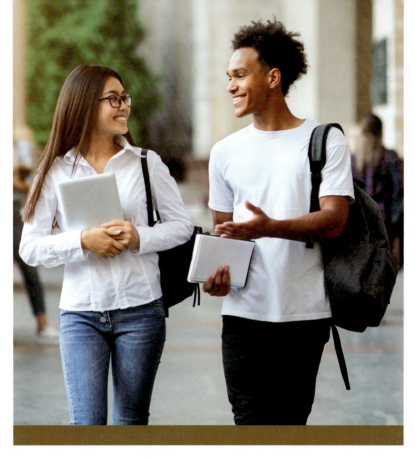

People who want to become industrial mechanics can get a two-year associate's degree from community college.

If a person trains to be a mechanic after high school, training usually lasts a year or more. This training can be done through a combination of coursework and workplace experiences. Becoming an industrial mechanic does not require a four-year college degree. However, some people get a two-year associate's degree. Their path usually depends on factors such as time, money, and personal preference.

There are different ways to become an industrial mechanic. Some people choose trade school or community college. Others apply for an apprenticeship. A training program is another option. Still others start from an entry level position and learn from a mentor. Mechanics who want more education can get certifications. This training can increase skills in specific industries, specialized machinery, or technology. Mechanics with advanced training may receive job promotions and better pay.

CHOOSING A PATH

Many people who want to become industrial mechanics go to trade school.

APPRENTICESHIP VS. TRADE SCHOOL

Choosing between an apprenticeship and trade school is a personal decision. Apprentices earn money while training, but their training tends to be more general. Trade school students can train with more specific technologies. Both options can lead to good careers in industrial mechanics.

Trade schools are also known as vocational schools or career and technical colleges. These schools offer classes and on-site experiences. Some schools offer two-year associate's degrees. This is a good option for those who want a diploma, a degree, or an industry certificate.

Students who want to earn money while going to school can apply for an apprenticeship. Eugene Scalia served as the US Secretary of Labor from 2019 to 2021. Scalia said, "Apprenticeships are widely recognized to be a highly effective job-training approach for . . . the

Apprenticeships can help people learn more about the job while they get paid.

skilled workforce."[4] Completing an apprenticeship can help students move into advanced careers.

Training programs offer a different path to becoming an industrial mechanic.

For example, the Universal Technical Institute has a training program for people interested in an industrial maintenance career. No experience is needed. Trainees learn how to use measuring devices used in the field. They learn about safety and electrical theory. People can complete the program in 30 to 39 weeks before going into the workforce.

Industry certifications help industrial mechanics learn new skills. People who want this kind of extra training are valued by employers. This shows dedication. For example, mechanics can become a

Certificates typically require taking exams.

certified vibration analyst. They are trained to find and correct vibrations that might cause machine failure. Other certifications include titles such as certified balancing specialist and fluid power engineer. Each of these has its own training and exam requirements. A certification is not necessary. However, certifications can help people move up in their careers.

SCHOLARSHIP PROGRAMS

Today there is a push to recognize the trades as a solid career choice. College is not for everyone. However, most of today's trade jobs require some training beyond high school.

Computer technology and robotics are found in many factories. Industrial mechanics must be able to work with these technologies. This may require advanced training. Sometimes a company will pay for employees to go to school.

Applying for scholarships can be beneficial for people who need extra money to go to trade school.

Other times, employees must pay for their own classes. If that is the case, trade scholarships can help with expenses.

Many scholarships are competitive. They are awarded to individuals with the best applications. Each scholarship has its own rules and requirements. It is important to research each one before applying.

People who get scholarships receive money to go to school. One popular scholarship opportunity is the DEWALT Trades Scholarship. High school seniors or graduates can apply. The scholarship is also available for college students. It is meant to help those who are interested in getting a degree or certificate in the trades. This includes fields like construction, carpentry, and machinery.

Those who meet the application deadline and requirements will receive scholarship money. For example, in 2022 the DEWALT Trades Scholarship offered up to forty scholarships of $5,000. Scholarships can help students learn the skills needed for today's job market.

HEROES MAKE AMERICA

Heroes MAKE America is committed to helping military personnel who are returning home. The Manufacturing Institute is the organization behind this program. It has helped many veterans find jobs in manufacturing. Many former military mechanics have found work as industrial mechanics through Heroes MAKE America.

CHAPTER THREE

WHAT IS LIFE LIKE AS AN INDUSTRIAL MECHANIC?

Industrial mechanics usually work for large manufacturing companies. They work regular daytime hours, which is usually a forty-hour work week. Overtime is often required because machines that break down must be fixed. This means

Industrial mechanics can run tests to make sure a machine is working properly.

that a mechanic will sometimes work more than forty hours. They will work until the job is finished. Mechanics have a list of jobs that must be completed every day. These include regular inspections and maintenance of machinery and equipment. However, when something breaks, the mechanic must stop everything to diagnose and fix the problem. This takes priority over everything else. Production must resume as quickly as possible.

Industrial mechanics often work in teams. Each team has a lead mechanic who has years of experience. The lead mechanic usually answers questions. He or she takes responsibility for the quality of the team's work.

An industrial mechanic's day might begin with a team meeting. Lead mechanics

Team meetings help mechanics stay on task.

go over the day's duties. They make sure everyone knows what to do. A regular maintenance schedule is followed. Every machine must be inspected and serviced. This helps prevent major problems.

Very large companies may have several teams of mechanics and technicians. Each team is responsible for a specific set of machines. They must communicate with each other to keep all areas running smoothly. A problem in one area will affect production in other areas.

Safety is very important for industrial mechanics. Working with large machines can be dangerous. This is why most companies have strict safety policies. Everyone must obey safety rules and regulations. Companies can be heavily fined if they are not following safety rules.

Wearing safety glasses and a hard hat can help prevent injuries.

Workers have the right to a safe and healthy work environment. If the company does not have a safe work environment, workers can file a complaint with the Occupational

Safety and Health Administration (OSHA). Once they do, workers can request an inspection.

The most common accident suffered by those working with industrial machines is being struck by an object. *USA Today*

THE OCCUPATIONAL SAFETY AND HEALTH ADMINISTRATION (OSHA)

OSHA is part of the US Department of Labor. It sets and enforces safety standards that must be followed by businesses. Industrial mechanics work around large equipment and must consider safety. Companies that do not comply with OSHA guidelines can get into legal trouble and pay heavy fines.

reported that in 2016 there were forty-five workers who died in accidents on the job. Another 4,490 workers were injured.

To prevent injury, mechanics need to make sure they have the right personal protective equipment (PPE). PPE can include work gloves, safety glasses, and masks. This is especially important if the mechanic is working with toxic chemicals. Hard hats and steel-toed shoes can help protect mechanics from falling objects. A mechanic should make sure they have extra PPE wherever they go. Companies and the mechanics must make safety a priority.

TOOLS OF THE TRADE

An industrial mechanic needs to be trained to use many kinds of tools. These include hand tools and power tools. Many power tools are powered by compressed air. Compressed air is created by forcing air into a small space. Releasing the air gives tools their power. These tools are called pneumatic tools. Pneumatic tools are commonly referred to as air-powered tools.

Some examples of pneumatic tools are wrenches and drills. A pneumatic wrench is used to tighten or loosen bolts.

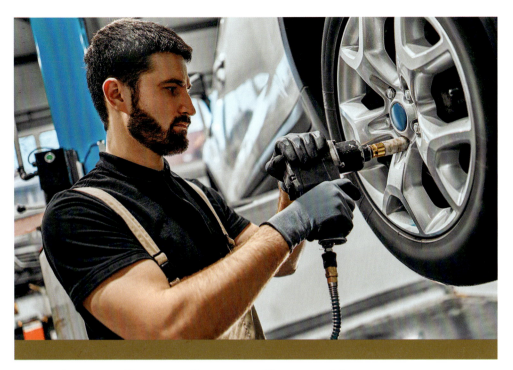

Pneumatic wrenches are often used in car shops, assembly lines, and heavy equipment manufacturing.

It is connected to an air compressor. The compressor powers the wrench with air. The force of the air allows the wrench to quickly tighten or loosen large bolts. Pneumatic tools are often lighter than electric tools. This is because they have

no heavy motors or large battery packs.
However, they are still powerful enough
to be dangerous. Workers must learn
and practice safety measures. They need
to wear protective equipment such as
eye goggles.

Mechanics need tools for testing, taking
measurements, **troubleshooting**, and
installation. They should know how to
read a scale, a ruler, and a tape measure.
Reading manuals and blueprints is also
part of the job. Mechanics often work with
welding equipment too. Some machinery
is controlled by a computer. Mechanics

working with computer-controlled machines must know how to enter instructions into the machine.

PERSONAL QUALITIES FOR SUCCESS

Successful industrial mechanics like working with their hands. The ability to work with small parts and tight spaces is important.

PROGRAMMABLE LOGIC CONTROLLERS (PLCs)

Modern factories use automation to speed up production. PLCs are tiny computers that are used for automation. They monitor machinery and provide information to industrial mechanics on the factory floor. Repairs and adjustments are made based on the information from the PLCs. This keeps things running smoothly and efficiently.

Physical strength is needed when lifting large parts of a machine. It is also required when moving heavy equipment.

No two days are alike for industrial mechanics. They may use small, delicate tools one day and then have to dismantle and move a large machine the next. Mechanics constantly need to adapt to changing demands.

Troubleshooting is another important skill. Observing and regularly maintaining machines are important responsibilities. Mechanics investigate problems when they happen. However, experienced mechanics

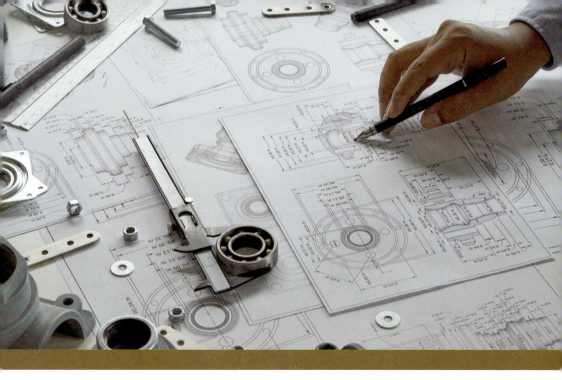

Troubleshooting problems can sometimes involve reading diagrams and instructions.

will think ahead. They will try to stop problems before they occur.

Industrial mechanics need to work well with others. There are often teams of mechanics and maintenance technicians. Oral communication is important when working in a team. Mechanics might

be asked for input about a machine.
They might also be asked how to
improve production. In these situations,
listening and asking questions can show
good communication skills. Written
communication is also important. This is
helpful when writing notes and emails to
other technicians.

A willingness to learn is an important
quality. This is especially relevant because
technology is always changing. Mechanics
must be willing to invest in additional
training. An interviewee in *Career as an
Industrial Maintenance Mechanic* stated,

Mechanics may need to know how to maintain and fix industrial robots.

"I've been in this field for two decades and I've seen a lot change. Most people assume that a mechanic's job is hard, dirty, greasy. That was back in the day. Today it's all about automation technology and career opportunities. Electronics play a huge role in industrial maintenance now."[5]

CHAPTER FOUR

WHAT IS THE FUTURE FOR INDUSTRIAL MECHANICS?

The Bureau of Labor Statistics (BLS) is a government agency. The BLS website keeps track of information about many different careers. Visitors to the site can learn all about any career. They can learn what life is like on the job. They learn

Many industrial mechanics work in large factories with a lot of machinery.

how much money they can earn. The website also tells users what the future looks like for a career. The BLS states, "Overall employment of industrial machinery mechanics, machinery maintenance workers, and millwrights is projected to grow 14 percent from 2021 to 2031, much faster than the average for all occupations."[6]

In 2021, there were 384,800 industrial mechanics. By 2031, the BLS expects there to be 447,900 of these jobs. Many companies are now using automated machinery in their plants. Mechanics will be needed to keep these machines running. Industrial mechanics will be important for many years to come.

Industrial mechanics make a good, stable income. However, pay varies by state and industry. Experience, training, and certifications also affect income level.

TOP PAYING AREAS FOR INDUSTRIAL MECHANICS

STATES	HOURLY WAGE	ANNUAL WAGE
HAWAII	$37.87	$78,780
ALASKA	$36.90	$76,740
DISTRICT OF COLUMBIA	$36.28	$75,470
WYOMING	$35.71	$74,270
CONNECTICUT	$31.82	$66,190

Source: "Occupational Employment and Wage Statistics," Bureau of Labor Statistics, May 2021. www.bls.gov.

The Bureau of Labor Statistics states that in May 2021, the nationwide average pay for an industrial mechanic was $59,380.

Many mechanics are part of labor unions. A labor union is an organization formed by workers in a particular trade or industry. Labor unions advocate for fair pay, benefits, and better working conditions.

The *Career as an Industrial Maintenance Mechanic* points out that the average wage difference between union and nonunion jobs is nearly 25 percent. That means a mechanic in a union can earn about $200 more per week or $10,000 more per year. Unions work out salaries for their workers by meeting with company leaders. They negotiate payment contracts.

Workers in unions typically make more money than those who are not in unions.

Though being part of a labor union sounds helpful, there are some drawbacks. Employees must pay union dues. This can sometimes be expensive. The union may also have rules for workers to follow. Unions also tend to favor seniority. The longer a worker has been around, the less likely they will be laid off or fired. That makes newer workers more likely to lose their jobs. Unions are a choice. They often improve working conditions. But there are downsides to working in a unionized company.

ADVANCES IN TECHNOLOGY

Technology is an important part of manufacturing. Large factories use automation to speed up production. Robots can be found in many packaging plants. They help people do tasks that are repetitive or dangerous. Robots can lift heavy loads and move materials quickly.

Some factories use robots to move heavy items like steel fences.

Artificial intelligence (AI) and **sensors** can be used to predict when a machine might break down. This helps mechanics fix problems before they occur.

3D printers can make tools and parts

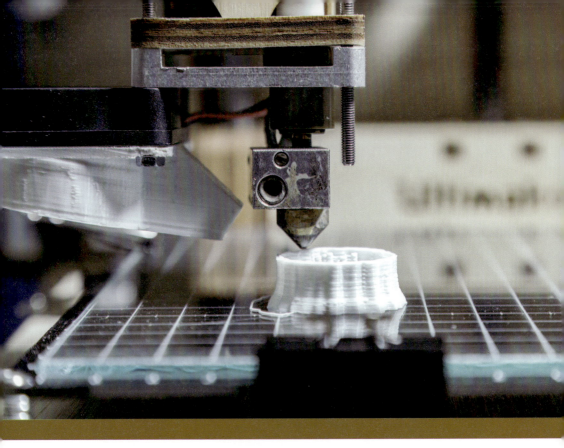

3D printers can make tools out of materials such as plastic, polymer powder, and metal.

for industrial machines. This can save a company both time and money.

The technology used is different for each industry. However, technology cannot replace the job of an industrial mechanic. Mechanics are still needed to maintain high-tech machinery. Training or certifications help mechanics work with new technologies.

MENTORING THE NEXT GENERATION

Becoming an industrial mechanic takes hard work. Connecting with mentors who know the job can make it easier. Apprentices are assigned to mentors in the work setting. Mentors help new mechanics learn and grow.

There are mentors outside of apprenticeships too. Many trade schools and technical colleges have mentoring programs. Mentors working in manufacturing connect with students.

They give advice and answer questions.

Sometimes they have students shadow

them on the job. This means that students

can follow and observe their mentors in

the workplace.

The state of Ohio started the Ohio

Manufacturing Mentorship Program. This

program wants to address the shortage

of workers in manufacturing. It helps

companies connect with local school

districts to find students interested in

these jobs. Students do not need to be

attending a technical education school.

Typically, mentors have worked in the field for many years.

They must be 16 or 17 years old. Before they start work, the students need to complete ten hours of safety training. They also need to learn about health hazards in the job. Afterward, they are assigned to a mentor. Students get to do part-time work with their mentors. Mentors teach their students how to use certain tools. Tools can include pipe and bolt threading machines. These machines cuts pipes cleanly and efficiently.

After completing the program, students can legally work in a manufacturing setting. Jim Scheuing, the general manager at Extrudex Aluminum, took part in this Ohio program. His experience with the students was very positive. He commented that students got more and more excited as they learned. He said, "It's nice to see young

More women are seeking careers in the skilled trades.

people that are looking for an industry and get started."[7]

WOMEN IN THE FIELD

Women make up 3.4 percent of all industrial mechanics. It is still considered a **nontraditional** job for women. This is because it is in an industry dominated by men. The industry is changing as many skilled jobs are going unfilled. This lack of skilled workers could become a crisis. Since women make up about half of the US workforce, they are being encouraged to explore careers in the skilled trades.

Traditional jobs for women often pay less than traditional jobs for men. Also, some women have experienced harassment by male coworkers. Women often must overcome a large learning curve. This is because they usually have to start from the beginning without knowing much about the job. However, these challenges can be overcome with the right support.

Today, some organizations work to support women in manufacturing. They offer mentorship and resources. They also provide opportunities for women to

WOMEN MAKE AMERICA

Women MAKE America wants to recruit 1,000 female mentors from 2022 to 2027 who will work with women in manufacturing. The organization believes that women benefit more by being mentored by other women in male-dominated trades.

connect with peers. Women MAKE America and Women in Apprenticeship and Nontraditional Occupations (WANTO) are two such organizations. They are successful programs that are making a difference for women working in the trades.

WANTO gives **grants** to organizations working to attract women into the trades. The Fresh Start Women's Foundation received a grant in 2022. This organization is based in Phoenix, Arizona. WANTO helped employers recruit and train women in jobs related to construction and information technology (IT). WANTO also

There are organizations that help train women to become industrial mechanics.

helped the foundation grow employment opportunities for women in Phoenix. It also financially supported women and their families. In the long run, organizations like these will help a city's economy.

A CAREER WITH A FUTURE

Industrial mechanics have an important job in a fast-growing industry. Because of them, manufacturers can produce the goods and services that we depend on to live, work, and play. Becoming an industrial mechanic means having a career with a bright future.

There is a high demand for industrial mechanics.

GLOSSARY

3D printers
printers that carry out instructions to create a three-dimensional object by layering heated plastic over and over until the object has been formed

artificial intelligence
the ability of a machine to imitate human intelligence

automated
operating according to programmed instructions

conveyors
machines that move materials from one place to the next

grants
money that an organization gives for a specific purpose

sensors
mechanical devices that take readings and measurements to provide information

troubleshooting
the act of finding the source of a problem so that it can be fixed

SOURCE NOTES

CHAPTER ONE: WHAT DOES AN INDUSTRIAL MECHANIC DO?

1. Quoted in "Frito Lay Industrial Mechanic Video," *YouTube*, uploaded by Houston County School District, January 20, 2017. www.youtube.com.

2. *Career as an Industrial Maintenance Mechanic*. Chicago: Institute for Career Research, 2012, p. 6.

3. Quoted in "Industrial Mechanic Youth Apprenticeship: Shannon Brennan," *YouTube*, uploaded by TridentTech, April 18, 2018. www.youtube.com.

CHAPTER TWO: WHAT TRAINING DO INDUSTRIAL MECHANICS NEED?

4. Quoted in "US Department of Labor Issues Industry-Recognized Apprenticeship Program Final Rule," *US Department of Labor*, March 10, 2020. www.dol.gov.

CHAPTER THREE: WHAT IS LIFE LIKE AS AN INDUSTRIAL MECHANIC?

5. *Career as an Industrial Maintenance Mechanic*, p. 8.

CHAPTER FOUR: WHAT IS THE FUTURE FOR INDUSTRIAL MECHANICS?

6. Quoted in "Industrial Machinery Mechanics, Machinery Maintenance Workers, and Millwrights," *US Bureau of Labor Statistics*, September 8, 2022. www.bls.gov.

7. Quoted in "Mentorship Program Available to High School Students and Manufacturers," *YouTube*, uploaded by commerceohio, October 1, 2021. www.youtube.com.

FOR FURTHER RESEARCH

BOOKS

S.L. Hamilton, *Industrial Robots*. Minneapolis, MN: Abdo Publishing, 2019.

Mary-Lane Kamberg, *Working with Tech in Manufacturing*. New York: Rosen Publishing, 2020.

Tom Streissguth, *Skilled Trades in the Military*. San Diego, CA: ReferencePoint Press, 2023.

INTERNET SOURCES

"5 Emerging Technologies for Manufacturing," *Association for Advancing Automation*, March 30, 2021. www.automate.org.

"The Evolution of Industrial Maintenance," *ATS*, n.d., www.advancedtech.com.

"What Is an Industrial Mechanic?" *Zippia*, n.d., www.zippia.com.

WEBSITES

ApprenticeshipUSA
www.apprenticeship.gov

ApprenticeshipUSA is an official government website that lists approved apprenticeships for vocational occupations. The website provides information about specific occupations as well as links to approved apprenticeships for those occupations.

Occupational Outlook Handbook
www.bls.gov

The Occupational Outlook Handbook is an online publication of the Bureau of Labor Statistics. The handbook provides a wealth of information about many different careers, including a career summary, work environment, pay, job outlook, and statistics.

O*Net Online
www.onetonline.org

O*Net Online has compiled nearly 1,000 career profiles. Users can read about each career as well as acquire information about education and certifications available.

INDEX

3D printers, 61

apprenticeships, 11, 22–25, 28, 29, 30–31, 63

artificial intelligence (AI), 61

Brennan, Shannon, 22–25

Bureau of Labor Statistics (BLS), 54–56, 57

Career as an Industrial Maintenance Mechanic, 20, 52, 58

certifications, 28, 32–34, 56, 63

DEWALT Trades Scholarship, 36

Fresh Start Women's Foundation, 70

General Education Development (GED), 26

Heroes MAKE America, 37

Hoffman, Craig H., 15

labor unions, 58–59

mentors, 28, 63–64, 66, 69

Occupational Safety and Health Administration (OSHA), 44

Ohio Manufacturing Mentorship Program, 64

personal protective equipment (PPE), 45

pneumatic tools, 46–48

programmable logic controllers (PLCs), 49

robots, 8, 16, 22, 34, 60

Rowe, Mike, 23

safety, 32, 42–45, 48, 65

Scalia, Eugene, 30

Scheuing, Jim, 66

scholarships, 23, 34–37

trade schools, 11, 28–30, 63

Universal Technical Institute, 32

US Department of Labor, 44

USA Today, 44

Women in Apprenticeship and Nontraditional Occupations (WANTO), 70

Women MAKE America, 69, 70

IMAGE CREDITS

Cover: © Pornpimon Rodchua/iStockphoto
5: © serts/iStockphoto
7: © Zulkarnieiev Denis/Shutterstock Images
9: © Roman Zaiets/Shutterstock Images
10: © Goroden Koff/Shutterstock Images
13: © Extreme-Photographer/iStockphoto
16: © Jasen Wright/Shutterstock Images
19: © NanoStockk/iStockphoto
21: © Ground Picture/Shutterstock Images
24: © serts/iStockphoto
27: © Prostock Studio/Shutterstock Images
31: © Rich Vintage/iStockphoto
33: © LStock Studio/Shutterstock Images
35: © FreshSplash/iStockphoto
39: © Kling Sup/Shutterstock Images
41: © Mungkhood Studio/Shutterstock Images
43: © Obradovic/iStockphoto
47: © Harbucks/Shutterstock Images
51: © Chaosamran Studio/iStockphoto
53: © Factory Easy/Shutterstock Images
55: © industryviews/Shutterstock Images
57: © Red Line Editorial
59: © Korn T/Shutterstock Images
61: © Juice Flair/Shutterstock Images
62: © Sergi Lopez Roig/Shutterstock Images
65: © industryview/iStockphoto
67: © skynesher/iStockphoto
71: © Amorn Suriyan/Shutterstock Images
73: © noomcpk/Shutterstock Images

ABOUT THE AUTHOR

Martha Hubbard is an Ohio-based author with a background in teaching and school librarianship. She is drawn to writing nonfiction because she loves to learn as much as she loves to write. She is married to her husband of 33 years and has two adult children. When she is not reading or writing, Martha loves to take long walks outdoors and spend time with her family and three dogs.